Outwardly
Active

Also by David Westlake

Upwardly Mobile

SOUL SURVIVOR PRESENTS

Outwardly Active

EVANGELISM AS JESUS DID IT

DAVID WESTLAKE

WITH CRAIG BORLASE

Hodder & Stoughton
LONDON SYDNEY AUCKLAND

Copyright © 2001 by David Westlake

First published in Great Britain in 2001

The right of David Westlake to be identified as the Author of
the Work has been asserted by him in accordance with
the Copyright, Designs and Patents Act 1988.

10 9 8 7 6 5 4 3 2 1

British Library Cataloguing in Publication Data
A record for this book is available from the British Library

ISBN 0 340 78556 X

Typeset by Avon Dataset Ltd, Bidford-on-Avon, Warks

Printed and bound in Great Britain by
Clays Ltd, St Ives plc

Hodder & Stoughton
A Division of Hodder Headline Ltd
338 Euston Road
London NW1 3BH

Contents

Foreword

Outwardly Active is part of a series of books from Soul Survivor that are written on crucial subjects and aimed particularly at Christian young people, to encourage them in their walks with Jesus and their witness of him.

David's first contribution to the series, *Upwardly Mobile*, was a wonderful book on sharing God's heart for the poor and issues of social justice. *Outwardly Active* surpasses even that in providing us with down-to-earth empowerment that you can really take up and apply to your everyday life.

This is a wonderful and liberating book that smashes all the stereotypes on evangelism. I found myself reading through its pages exclaiming, 'Yes,' 'Yes!', 'YES!' as I read stuff that made sense, and sighed with relief as I came away from it each time thinking, 'Phew, so I don't have to do it like that!'

Dave writes with tremendous insights, deep conviction and more than a touch of humour as he takes us through his personal experiences and biblical references in order to equip us for a lifestyle of evangelism. It's not a call to be something you're not; this won't burden you with unnatural expressions of being a Christian. It pulls us away from the sales pitch and takes us to the heart of who we are in Jesus, sharing the Son of God through friendships and relationships in real life. What's more, I know Dave and I know that all that he writes about, he actually does. Knowing the integrity with which this book is written makes it even more compelling a read!

I can't recommend this book highly enough. We're delighted to have this book in this series. And I can't wait to see its effects as it gets out into the hands of young people and to see the difference it makes as you find forms of sharing Jesus that are natural to you. Ponder its sanctified common sense and find yourself living 'evangelism' as they did in the early Church.

Mike Pilavachi
April 2001

Introduction

If you've picked up a book as thin as this on evangelism, you're clearly on the hunt for something special: evangelism*lite*, diet evangelism or something similarly short, sharp and relatively harmless to your everyday life, some quick way out that's decidedly low on pain and misery. Let's face it, to be writing a book as thin as this on evangelism hardly places me in the Plenty To Say camp when it comes to the subject. So let's just get all that tricky stuff out the way right now, shall we? Here goes: I don't like evangelism. For me it's like the male menopause come early, leaving me lilting from the hot flushes, retching from the stomach churnings and weeping from embarrassment at some of my more 'imaginative' behaviour. But you know the worst thing about it? Unlike the marching on of time and the body's changes, to me evangelism feels anything but natural. It feels like a game I never understood, never mastered and never wanted to play again.

You see, I just feel awkward about it. No matter how hard I try, it's impossible for me to divorce the internal reaction that says 'AAAAAAAAAAAAAAAAAAAGH' whenever I find myself coming face to face with this thing called evangelism. Take last summer, for instance. I was at a conference with plenty of other people, getting nice and excited about the prospect of hitting the streets in the afternoon and spreading a little bit of that Christianity = Good News stuff to the poor unsuspecting people in the streets. I was there, singing away about how great it all was, urging God to make 'salvation spring up from the ground', getting nice and sweaty from all that jumping up and down. In short, I was up for it. But then I got outside, made my way to one of the café venues, and it all changed. I felt timid, awkward and sick. If they'd asked me to get up on the stage and say something about how great Jesus is I would have done it like a shot, but walk over and chat to a group of people looking bewildered in the corner – well, that was a different story altogether.

To start off a conversation with a non-Christian often seems to set off a chain reaction in my head: they'll reject me . . . I'll look stupid . . . they won't be interested . . . what on earth do I say? And do you know what that reminds me of? Lisa Jones. You see, I liked Lisa a lot. As far as I was concerned, throughout my final year at primary school I was only minutes away from securing the young lady as my wife. But there was just one problem: every time I moved in to start up The Conversation with her, I froze.

In fact, I've never been one for chat-up lines. Come to think of it, that whole 'my, my, little lady, what's a nice girl like you . . .' thing seems to be outdated, irrelevant and wholly unworkable. Pulling by means of The Chat-Up Line does, after all, seem so *frightfully* passé, don't you think?

I've never been a happy fan of chat-up lines, so I'm willing to admit that my opinion on this matter may be a little one-sided, but talking to others it occurs to me that I might not be alone in feeling like this. Along with perhaps you, too, I just can't shake the feeling that whenever I try to hype myself up to perform the necessary evangelistic duties, I'm transporting myself back to the rear of the school hall and trying to figure out the magic password that will unlock the key to young Lisa Jones' heart. No wonder I feel nervous.

But I can't ignore the fact that when I was at the conference last summer, I was fully fired up about the importance of the whole church getting out there to tell and show people about Jesus. As an idea I think it's one of the better ones around, and I'm right behind it. Or at least I am right up until the moment I have to step out of the crowd and chat.

Why? Am I just shirking my responsibility? Am I putting my faith at the bottom of the pile simply because I feel a little shy or want to preserve my undeniably impressive street cred? Perhaps there is a little of that selfishness tucked away somewhere, but I'm wondering whether

that just might be all too neat, all too cosy an
answer. You see, if we're going to engage in any
kind of meaningful debate about the hows and
whys of Christianity, we have to be prepared to
ask some potentially awkward questions. Why?
Because, as the good book says, 'without vision
the people perish'. While I can't speak for you, I
know that I'm in serious need of some refinement
to my vision about just what it is I should be
doing when it comes to evangelism.

But enough of a warm-up; let's get down to
business. I've got a sneaking suspicion that in the
church today our whole approach to evangelism
is out of sync with the model offered us not only
by Jesus, but by the early church as well. That
very word – 'evangelism' – has become so tied up
with concepts of pressure, sales, baggage and
showmanship that we have forgotten the early
lessons handed down from the infant church.

With the developed world so bound up
by capitalism – by the ebbs and flows of
consumerism and the language of the contract
– it's perhaps not surprising that the church
has absorbed a little of its influence, but the
consequences have been drastic.

First of all, it has brought us to the point where

books like this are being written. Like checking your bank statements meticulously, evangelism has become for some people one of those chores that gets done only when we can't avoid it. Second, we've managed to contort the act of spreading the news about Jesus into a bizarre type of transaction. Like the salesperson asking us to switch gas or electricity suppliers, we might think that the best way to go about the whole business is to outline the relative benefits of Christianity, highlight some of the contractual obligations and ask people to make a quick decision, signing on the dotted line.

But is that really what Jesus had in mind when he delivered the granddaddy of pep-talks (also known as the Great Commission)? Did he really urge those gathered to 'go out and get as many converts as possible'? Was he considering introducing an incentive scheme that rewarded those who converted considerable numbers of people? Did he flirt with the idea of paying commission?

The truth is thankfully a little more complex. Where we have whittled down the 'go and make disciples of all nations' (Matt. 28:19) to 'go and *persuade* people to say a prayer of acceptance',

Jesus' original words ring loud with the sound of a deeper conviction. The game plan that he laid out before his disciples was simple: go and form relationships with others that are similar to those I have formed with you. Jesus was not after hordes of people to sign on the dotted line; he was looking for apprentices, people who were up for becoming like him through a process of spending time with him. Far from being the ultimate salesperson, Jesus wanted to bring many people into a relationship with God, not clinch as many five-minute soul-deals as possible. Let's be honest here: if evangelistic success comes primarily in the form of big rallies with big crowds making quick commitments, then Jesus' end-of-term report would surely have been stamped with the words 'could try harder'. After all, not only did he spend less than 10 per cent of his life in public ministry, but the accounts of the Gospels show him repeatedly putting most of his effort into the relationships found within his small group of disciples.

Before we slip headfirst into a sea of assumptions and anger, perhaps it might be worthwhile clearing up a few definitions. First, what do we mean by evangelism? It would seem that there are two types, both of vital importance to the continuing work laid down for us by Jesus. On the one hand is corporate evangelism and on the other is personal evangelism. Under the banner of the corporate flavour can be found all those large-scale events, winning arguments and persuasive personalities. Here we find those with a direct calling to be evangelists, those who – to use a farming metaphor – do the reaping. But as you can guess, all this corporate stuff is lifeless and stale unless it works in harmony with the personal evangelism that all Christians have a responsibility towards. For too long we have considered that personal evangelism is just the same as corporate evangelism without a microphone, but if we are ever going to be anything other than awkward and uncomfortable around evangelism then we must wise up to the truth. Personal evangelism marches to the beat of a different drum, one that connects with individuals, forms relationships and remains in it for the long haul rather than the quick fix. In other words, personal evangelism is all about discipleship.

Second, it's vital that we get this one point clear: those big gigs, the wholesale reapings, are fundamentally important. This book does not exist to sweep them under the carpet or declare that their days are numbered. Why, some of my best friends are evangelists. What we shall be looking at here are the issues that affect the rest of us, the way we can be outwardly active – and not just when our arm has been twisted so far behind our back that we have no option but to comply. What we shall be looking at is how our everyday actions can become channels through which we can fulfil Jesus' Great Commission. What we are talking about, in short, is lifestyle.

Want to know something special about Jesus? He didn't 'do' things to people: he had a relationship with people. Looking at the Bible it appears that Jesus' aim was not so much to put on a dazzling show that produced plenty of 'oohs' and 'aaaahs' from the open-mouthed crowd. No, he spoke to people, like the woman at the well, like Nicodemus, Zacchaeus, the rich young ruler and so on. He was so able to connect with people that it was through his relationships with them that he was able to work most profoundly. As we shall see, Jesus' model was so very different to our modern-day spiritual sales pitch.

It was about four years ago and I was walking

through Leicester Square. I had nothing particularly pressing to make my walk anything other than a stroll, and I paused to join a knot of people watching some act or other. It turned out that this was no mime, juggling or stand-up street performer, but a group of Christians presenting some street evangelism.

Midway through watching a piece about a body-builder who was able to bench-press a particularly heavy weight named 'sin', I was tapped on the shoulder by a young man. He was short, fresh-faced and wore a permanent half-smile. He was also keen. Very keen.

'So, you like the drama do you?'

'Oh yes,' I replied, not wanting to hurt his feelings. 'It's very thought-provoking.'

'I wonder if you've ever thought about hell, then.'

I must admit this one had me surprised. Sure, I was expecting some kind of jump into the deep end, but not for the water to be quite that cold. I recovered enough to explain that, yes, I had thought about hell because I too was a Christian.

Unfortunately, this answer – despite the fact that I was convinced it was a pretty good one – failed in its attempt to break the young man's stare and allow me on my way. Oh no. As far as he was concerned (and I know exactly what he was concerned about as he spent the next ten minutes explaining it all to me), I was not yet in the book of life. I tried to work out why that was so, and could only conclude that my imminent eternal torture in hell could only be avoided if I actually got down on my knees and allow him to personally witness my salvation being secured there and then. So I did. I said 'the prayer' and went on my way, leaving him a happy man and myself feeling dirty, used and worthless.

I suppose the really interesting thing about what happened to me that day was that the keen evangelist had given me an entirely correct gospel presentation. There were no grey areas, and he covered more than the basics of some of those key issues like sin, redemption, eternal life and Jesus' sacrifice. But despite this technical excellence he completely failed to connect with me as a person. It was evangelism in the style of telemarketing, and it did me no favours whatsoever.

If I had to isolate one thing about God that stands out above all the other things that amaze and astound me, it would have to be this: with him, it's all about relationships. If you look at the Trinity it is a perfect picture of a dynamic, integrated relationship. At the very core of our concept of God is the belief that he is a they, that Father, Son and Holy Spirit all exist in complete unity. A difficult concept for us to grasp, perhaps, but the language of the Bible underlines the message at regular intervals. The idea of eternal life is expressed as 'knowing God', and Jesus made a clear point of calling those who signed up to follow him 'sons and daughters'. Wherever you look, the message that God offers all the chance of being part of his family is never far away.

Strangely, it has been known for many in the church to develop selective amnesia when it comes to this point: we may acknowledge that God urges *us* to develop a relationship with him, but when it comes to how we treat others – well, that's a different matter altogether. You see, many of us have been guilty of becoming so wrapped up in getting people into the kingdom of God through logic, water-tight arguments or threats of violence that we have completely forgotten the relationship model as shown so clearly by Jesus himself.

Thinking about the differences between the

way Jesus went about his business and the way we go about it, there is another point that begs to be taken note of: Jesus didn't seem to have an 'us' and 'them' attitude, he didn't push people away. Of course, those who met him had the option of rejecting him for themselves, but turning his own back on others was something that Jesus never did. It appears to me that Jesus' default setting was that people were always in with him unless – like some of the Pharisees – they chose by their heart or their actions to reject him for themselves. This is the way that it is with God; his desire for relationship with us is so strong that it is us who push ourselves away from him rather than he who cuts himself off from us.

But what on earth does all this have to do with evangelism? Where is the connection between this and standing in Leicester Square performing street theatre to the unenlightened masses? In fact, it has plenty to do with all that stuff, because when we re-focus our view of how God sees the world, by extension it alters the way that we view it, too.

Of course, this doesn't mean that we create a picture of Jesus as some socially awkward pushover who was nice to all people in the hope that they would like him back. The Gospel accounts of Jesus' own life clearly indicate that he was able to be harsh with people in ways that might even make us blush now. It was often those top-notch religious types, the Pharisees, who incurred his anger, particularly as they distorted, polluted and hijacked the whole business of living a life of worship to God. But it is important to be clear; it was their behaviour that led them away from Jesus, not his desire for a cosy clique that kept them from coming in.

So how's about this for an idea: let's stop trying to be evangelists. In the way that we have come to define it – the slick presentations, the logical arguments, the very concept of going out and 'doing some evangelism' as if there is a switch within us that can turn our outreach activities on or off – let's give it a rest. Of course, we should continue to embrace corporate evangelism – the outreach meetings and so on – but when it comes down to the issue of how we live our lives, isn't it about time we tried something new? Let's face it, as an army of spiritual salespeople we are neither successful nor motivated. Let's get outwardly active.

Ah yes, you might be saying, it's all very well

chucking in a phrase like that, but what does it actually mean? To me, the main aim is that we learn how to live lives that are distinctively different, lives that are focused on relationships, lives that follow the Jesus model. Of course, we'll return to many of the activities that fit into the more traditional model of evangelism, revisiting, reviewing and refurbishing them in the light of a new approach. But for a while let's leave it all behind, all the sales, the hype, the system, the pressure, the desire for mass conversions rather than quality discipleship. Instead, let's see if we can't go about living a life that disturbs people, one that causes them to ask questions about why we are kind, why we are patient, self-sacrificing, generous and liberating. And let's get on and form relationships.

A final word. D. L. Moody, one of the best-known evangelists, was once presented with a very high-handed criticism of his missions. Replying about his evangelistic techniques he commented, 'Frankly, sir, I prefer the way that I do it to the way that you don't.' While the more traditional model of evangelism might not work for all of us, at least there are plenty around us who are having a go. I can find it all too easy to sit back, be cynically ironic and criticise all those whose style may not quite fit in with my own. But at least they're having a go. As Paul said, it's good 'to rejoice whenever [we] hear of the gospel being preached'. Perhaps we need to take this whole subject of evangelism to pieces in order to find out how it works, but as we do so, it is important to remember that leaving it in pieces on the floor and choosing to do nothing is not an option.

1

The Jesus Model

We like to be clear about the membership rules of this particular club. Let's face facts, becoming a Christian is relatively easy – just a matter of saying a few words and signing on the dotted line – but keeping things ticking over once you're on the inside, well, that can be another matter altogether. The truth is that we are far more concerned about who is in and who is out than it would appear Jesus was. While it might hurt us to admit it, we've managed to reduce the radical, politically dangerous movement that was the early church to a country club for people who don't like to get out too much.

This shift in attitude has affected the way we view those new recruits who come through the door. The way we welcome, explain, train and nurture those who are new to the faith is all based on a clear structure of progression: people arrive as non-Christians, they become Christians once they have said The Prayer, and from then on the road to spiritual maturity is littered with all manner of signposts, from baptism (with water and the Holy Spirit) to taking on positions of responsibility within the church. But when we turn to the Gospels, something rather frustrating happens. There is no clearly delineated and intricately defined ten-step programme towards becoming a full-on Christian. There do not appear to be any distinctions between Jesus' acts of evangelism, discipleship, healing and friendship. There are no lines like:

> . . . and then Jesus went to Capernaum where he held a five-day evangelistic mission, and they got a band in. After that he worked with the drama company on

their performance pieces. When he had
finished showing them how to mime being
locked in a room without a door, he moved
on to Sidon where he held a Bible week for
all the new believers.

The omission of anything like the above is a
bit of a shame, because I wonder whether this
Christian life thing would have been a whole lot
easier had Jesus followed the plan. If he had
simply left behind a nicely bound training manual complete with scripts, tests and a certificate
at the end that proved we've done things just
right, we could have got on with the job of simply
being a Christian without having to go through
that whole frustrating process of having to *think*
about what it means as well.

But he didn't leave such an induction pack,
and I believe that it wouldn't be too risky to
assume that this was not due to any failing on
his part. What we end up with – when we take
the time to look – is a startling revelation: there
were no clear lines between which of his followers
were in and which were out. With many of the
people who appear in the Gospels it can be
difficult to say with any sense of certainty

whether or not they are Christians at any given point. While there are a handful of situations where it is clear about their position, for the majority the whole issue of salvation is a little bit of a grey area. Which is why taking time to draw out some key distinctives about how Jesus interacted with people seems like a sound place to start.

JESUS' CALLING

The next day Jesus decided to leave for Galilee. Finding Philip, he said to him, 'Follow me.' Philip, like Andrew and Peter, was from the town of Bethsaida. Philip found Nathanael and told him, 'We have found the one Moses wrote about in the Law, and about whom the prophets also wrote — Jesus of Nazareth, the son of Joseph.'

'Nazareth! Can anything good come from there?' Nathanael asked.

'Come and see,' said Philip.

When Jesus saw Nathanael approaching, he said of him, 'Here is a true Israelite, in whom there is nothing false.'

'How do you know me?' Nathanael asked.

Jesus answered, 'I saw you while you were

still under the fig-tree before Philip called
you.'

Then Nathanael declared, 'Rabbi, you are
the Son of God; you are the King of Israel.'

Jesus said, 'You believe because I told you
I saw you under the fig-tree. You shall see
greater things than that.' He then added, 'I
tell you the truth, you shall see heaven
open, and the angels of God ascending and
descending on the Son of Man.'

(John 1:43–51)

Jesus' interaction here with just two of the eventual twelve disciples starts off with an interesting
point: Jesus called them to himself. Philip is
not told to follow Jesus' teaching, his ethical
standards or his flair for public spectacles; he
is told to follow Jesus. As we have established
already, the relationship on offer between us and
the creator of heaven is the key to Christianity,
the block on which all the rest stands.

For many of us, evangelism has rightly meant
imitating Jesus' approach and encouraging others
to establish their own relationship with him. But
in our attempt to do the right thing, could we be
taking it a little too literally? Perhaps there is
room for the argument that, like Jesus, we too

need to start out by offering a relationship to others, although making clear that it is a relationship with ourselves, too. You see, in ushering people straight on into a relationship with Jesus and standing back ourselves, we run the risk of giving off a message that clearly states it is not our intention to become contaminated by contact with the ungodly masses. 'Come and meet Jesus,' we proclaim with enthusiasm and joy, 'but don't even think about having me like and get to know you.' It is this attitude that can leave those on the receiving end of our evangelistic efforts with the feeling that they are just another consumer receiving just another sales pitch. Like the pumped-up telesalesperson, all that matters is clinching the deal; the rest is irrelevant.

There were three ways in which Jesus called people to get involved in a relationship with him. First, there was the more traditional, evangelistic approach that he used with Philip (having looked for him, Jesus came straight out with it). This ties in with our idea of the well-planned approach, where we manipulate a situation to introduce our topic of choice. And there's nothing wrong with it at all.

The second way in which Jesus laid down the

offer of getting to know him was by leaning on a more supernatural method of approach. Again we can see it in the passage above, as Jesus' conversation with Nathanael illustrates. By knowing what he was not supposed to know, Jesus allowed some of his own godliness to shine through, galvanising Nathanael's attention and blowing away his doubt and cynicism with a couple of simple sentences. Jesus' reliance on the supernatural gives us a clear indication about the direction that we might like to take, too: working in partnership with the Holy Spirit. We may think that we have all the answers for each conversation carried out within a relationship, but are we really so sure that we have no need of a little extra godly help?

Third, Jesus at times adopted a different approach altogether. We read that soon after he had met James, John, Peter and Andrew for the first time, he was simply hanging out with his new friends at Simon and Andrew's family home. Doing what, you may ask. Not much. Just spending time making friends with people. The story can be found towards the end of Mark 1, and the way it is written makes it seem like the most natural thing in the world for Jesus to be with them all, as natural as healing Peter's mother-in-law and as natural as chatting with the rest of the interested parties from the village. We have a knack of missing out this approach when we plan our high-profile evangelistic missions. After all, it takes too long, involves so much effort and can so easily produce very little in the way of tangible results. Yet we cannot deny that it works, as the popularity of the Alpha course clearly shows. There, the guiding principle is 'let's be nice to people', a concept that sadly has been sorely lacking from our strategies.

Take a look over the passage of scripture from John again and look at the language that Jesus uses: 'I saw you . . . You believe because I told you I saw you . . . You shall see . . . I tell you the truth, you shall see heaven open.' All those 'I's and 'you's go to saturate the passage with a sense that Jesus was fully plugged into the idea of establishing a personal relationship. There are no illustrations, no parables, just plain truth and revelation wrapped up in the offer to go and follow Jesus.

But what exactly did it mean when Jesus asked them to follow him? Wasn't this an example of just another deal being struck, another contract being signed? In truth, the words spoken by Jesus were linked to a change of lifestyle in a way that many of us would find difficult to comprehend. Where, to a new Christian today, following Jesus might mean saying regular prayers and attending church a couple of times a week, with Jesus a couple of millennia ago it took on a slightly more hefty tone. Following meant getting involved in an active relationship. It meant following physically, but it meant committing emotionally as well, just as Jesus was committed to them.

So it is clear that a relationship with Jesus has to start somewhere, and the three examples shown here – like the countless others found throughout the rest of the Gospels – show that Jesus often made the first move. There was the straight-out chat, the supernatural attention-grabber and the slow-burning relationship, each of which are certainly compatible with our own lives. OK, so perhaps walking up to a stranger and telling them to follow Jesus might seem like a bit of a regression to evangelism-as-a-way-of-torture, but is that really the message that we should be taking from the tale? Isn't it more a case that Jesus' approach to Philip indicates that people who don't yet know Jesus can still be

involved with him? After all, do people really
have to become Christians *before* we allow them
to join in on our social action projects? What
about having them come along anyway? Isn't that
what happened with Philip? We know that he
may have spent a fair bit of time around John
the Baptist, so Jesus' approach would not have
been totally out of the blue, but nevertheless
Philip was still offered the chance to take part in
a relationship long before he had established his
credentials as a trustworthy follower. Can you
imagine how an approach like that would look if
we were to apply it to the church today? Consider
the difference if, instead of making them sit
nicely in the pews while we lectured/entertained
them into submission, our non-Christian
friends were taking part in the life of the church,
contributing to the extending of the kingdom of
God.

JESUS' COMPANIONSHIP

Jesus shared his life with the disciples. For the
years they were together, their lives were inter-
twined as they ate, slept, travelled and worked as
a team. So often we read about Jesus turning to
them and explaining some profound truth as

they walked, or sitting them down to tackle a specific subject. There are instances where he helped them out practically – like paying Peter's taxes, feeding them or washing their feet – and occasions where he trained them, preparing them with tips and advice as they approached a specific town in which they were going to work. In other words, out of Jesus' calling to a relationship there came a companionship. And not an inconsistent type of companionship either, one where the earth was promised and barely anything was delivered. What Jesus promised was followed through. There were no disappointed tales from those who were on the sidelines after being cast off and thrown out of favour.

So what do we take from Jesus' model of companionship? At the centre is the vital importance of us learning to call people into a relationship with ourselves and, through us, with God. By getting to know us they get to see what we're like: who we are, what we value and where we're going. Of course, that might turn them right off, but surely such honesty is worth the risk?

As a youth worker I met a couple of people who stick out in my memory even now. Years have passed but I can still remember them coming round to my house, us getting to know each other and it all being very nice. And then I can remember the fear. One day they asked me what I was doing that evening and I briefly mentioned that I was off to a prayer meeting.

'Oh, that's OK,' said one of them, 'we'll come too.'

Ah. Problem. These people were not Christians. In fact, they were so very much not Christians that there was a very real danger that they would reduce certain participants at the prayer meeting to tears simply by opening their mouths. Not that they were nasty or malicious – far from it. It's just that they had no concept of the way we Christians behave. If these two were a work in progress, then it didn't take a genius to figure out that I had an awful lot more progress to make with them before they were fit for active service.

But they were insistent, and I became more terrified as the meeting approached. I knew there was no way I could turn them down, but the fear about what they might do, say or set fire to weighed heavy in my soul. Still, I knew it was right, particularly as I'd not evangelised them or tried to force them to join me; they were simply my friends and they wanted to do what I was doing that night. So we arrived, got on with the meeting and I felt mildly happier. Until they started smoking. Not that it was a major deal, but I did regret the fact that I hadn't pointed out that, as a rule, it wasn't the most typical tool for intercession. And then they got a bit bored and started to play their Walkmans. I cast an eye around the rest of the people at the meeting: it was clear that half of them were scandalised that such irreverent behaviour should be taking place in God's house, while the other half were wishing that they'd thought of it themselves a little earlier.

But they came back. Week after week they wanted to be there, still smoking, still listening to their Walkmans in the boring bits. Then one day one of them spoke out during a lull in the prayers.

'I'll pray now,' he said.

I nodded at him, and we waited.

'I want to ask God to be nice to us. How do I do that?'

'You just tell that to God,' I said.

And he did. When he had finished and said amen, he got a particularly loud chorus of amens as everyone was well excited that a non-Christian was praying nice things in our meeting. And he felt good. He felt included. He felt part of what we were doing.

Before we sign to the belief that the aim is to get non-Christians to feel comfortable within our own meetings and infrastructure, it might be worth taking a quick look back at the Gospels. There we see plenty of instances where Jesus' offer of companionship can be found in the most mundane of settings. Take the calling of Levi, for example:

Once again Jesus went out beside the lake. A large crowd came to him, and he began to teach them. As he walked along, he saw Levi son of Alphaeus sitting at the tax collector's booth. 'Follow me,' Jesus told him, and Levi got up and followed him.

While Jesus was having dinner at Levi's house, many tax collectors and 'sinners' were eating with him and his disciples, for there were many who followed him. When the teachers of the law who were Pharisees saw him eating with the 'sinners' and tax collectors, they asked his disciples: 'Why does he eat with tax collectors and "sinners"?'

On hearing this, Jesus said to them, 'It is not the healthy who need a doctor, but the sick. I have not come to call the righteous, but sinners.'

Mark 2:13–17

Has it ever struck you *where* it was that Jesus wanted Levi to follow him to? It's there in the text, but too often we can gloss over the fact that the next line tells us that Jesus was having dinner *chez* Levi. His companionship worked both home and away, on the safe ground of an established group of friends and in the relative uncertainty of a stranger's house. No matter what the context, it is clear that Jesus and those with whom he was sharing companionship were able to find common ground.

The story of Jesus meeting Zacchaeus takes this further, as Luke 19 points out:

Jesus entered Jericho and was passing through. A man was there by the name of Zacchaeus; he was a chief tax collector and was wealthy. He wanted to see who Jesus was, but being a short man he could not, because of the crowd. So he ran ahead and climbed a sycamore-fig tree to see him, since Jesus was coming that way.

When Jesus reached the spot, he looked up and said to him, 'Zacchaeus, come down immediately. I must stay at your house today.' So he came down at once and welcomed him gladly. All the people saw this and began to mutter, 'He has gone to be the guest of a "sinner".'

But Zacchaeus stood up and said to the Lord, 'Look, Lord! Here and now I give half of my possessions to the poor, and if I have cheated anybody out of anything, I will pay back four times the amount.'

Jesus said to him, 'Today salvation has come to this house, because this man, too, is a son of Abraham. For the Son of Man came to seek and to save what was lost.'

Luke 19:1–10

Again we see that when Jesus called someone, he did it for the purpose of friendship. In the same way as he led Levi back to his house for a spot of supper and a direct revelation about the nature of salvation, Jesus called Zacchaeus down from the tree so that they might spend a little time together. And of course, the truly cute thing about the Zacchaeus story is the ending; Zacchaeus has a tangible change of heart and becomes a force for justice in the area. To take a little poetic licence, can you imagine what happened before Zacchaeus addressed the crowd? Was Jesus coaching him discreetly in the house, writing his speech and helping him to deliver it in an oh-so-sincere way? Of course not. Which leads us to the logical conclusion that merely by spending time with Jesus Zacchaeus' whole life was turned upside down.

Yet we know that at times Jesus was abundantly clear about where people were going wrong. He may not have given Zacchaeus a verbal beating about his wayward lifestyle as he clambered down from the tree, but he certainly pulled no punches when it came to addressing the Pharisees. Those religious types who really should have known better received the full lashing of his scorn, being labelled 'whitewashed tombs' and so on.

From these stories and others, I wonder whether we can suggest that Jesus was as concerned that people knew about his offer of companionship as that they knew about their own sin. In other words, I don't believe that he was so afraid of sin that it stopped people becoming his friend.

JESUS' CONVICTION

Before we slide off into a free-for-all of self-denial and indulgence, concluding that all Jesus ever wants to do is tell us we're very lovely and not to get too bothered about all that messy sin stuff, it's worth being clear about another phase that Jesus' relationships went through. The plain and simple truth is that Jesus managed to hold the balance between offering companionship and convicting people of the harsh realities of their less-than-godly lifestyles. Jesus brought truth into people's lives, uncomfortable as it may have been.

I once did some training with a group of youth workers who were involved with people right on the fringes of society. These young people had been rejected by everyone, and the team who were working alongside them had managed to scale seeming mountains by securing their trust and earning their friendship. It was inspiring stuff, but there was a problem which was evident to all involved: nothing was changing in the young people's lives. These sacrificial youth

workers had become so good at offering uncon-
ditional friendship that the language of Jesus'
conviction had slipped from their vocabulary. To
say that we are sinful and do need to turn around
might not be the most user-friendly way of going
about things; it may stick in our throat and leave
both parties feeling a little bit the worse for wear.
Yet is that the only option? Is sending people on
some serious guilt trip the only way we can help
people get to know Jesus better?

The way Jesus did it was special. He secured
people's interest and inspired them to change
through stories and parables. And it took time.

In Matthew chapter 16 we have a snapshot of
the moment that the penny dropped for Peter:

When Jesus came to the region of Caesarea
Philippi, he asked his disciples, 'Who do
people say the Son of Man is?'

They replied, 'Some say John the Baptist;
others say Elijah; and still others, Jeremiah
or one of the prophets.'

'But what about you?' he asked. 'Who do
you say I am?'

Simon Peter answered, 'You are the
Christ, the Son of the living God.'

Jesus replied, 'Blessed are you, Simon son

of Jonah, for this was not revealed to you by man, but by my Father in heaven. And I tell you that you are Peter, and on this rock I will build my church, and the gates of Hades will not overcome it. I will give you the keys of the kingdom of heaven; whatever you bind on earth will be bound in heaven, and whatever you loose on earth will be loosed in heaven.' Then he warned his disciples not to tell anyone that he was the Christ.

Matthew 16:13–20

Peter's line about Jesus being the Son of God is truly remarkable, for this simple reason: he first met Jesus back in chapter 4, receiving the call while he was mending his fishing nets. So that's twelve chapters of hanging around Jesus, twelve chapters of being a vital part of the team, twelve chapters of being trusted and being sent off to drive out evil spirits and heal the sick. To an outsider Peter was one of the key players in the Jesus squad. He was there as Jesus went about his business, and the assumptions that would have been made about Peter's own spiritual state would surely have been far from accurate. Yet all of this responsibility, all of this activity, comes before Peter sees who Jesus really is, before he twigs that Jesus really is the Son of God, before he gets saved.

I heard it said that when it comes to issues like this, what matters most is our motion towards rather than our actual destination. In other words, we will never be convicted enough, we will never reach a point of being able to say, 'Yup, I'm as godly a person as I need to be.' What is important is that we encourage each other to keep on heading in the right direction. After all, isn't that precisely the case with Peter? For twelve chapters he was most definitely not up there with the most enlightened and certified of Jesus' followers – by today's standards he'd still be making up his mind at the back of the meetings, months away from taking on any sort of responsibility within the church. Yet he was accepted, trusted and depended upon even while he was on the early stage of his journey.

Too often we think of conviction as a rite of passage, a point in our early spiritual development that marks us either in or out of a relationship with Jesus. While that might make it easier to control the life of the church, it unfortunately fails to fall into line with Jesus' way of doing things. He was clearly happy to have people identify with him who were making their way into the kingdom, not just those who were there already.

To return to that old chestnut of a Sunday school story – Zacchaeus – it strikes me that something bizarre happened that gives us an insight into the way Jesus discipled people. Zacchaeus obviously knew something about Jesus, or at least he knew enough to fire his curiosity to the extent that he climbed the tree to view the parade. Yet knowing *about* Jesus was clearly not having a huge effect on his life, or at least the results of it paled into insignificance when compared with how things changed for him once he actually *met* Jesus. It was only once he had spent time in his presence that Zacchaeus' behaviour proved that 'Today salvation has come to this house.'

To return to Peter's penny-dropping moment in Matthew 16, we can question why Jesus chose that particular moment to convict Peter of his true identity. The answer has to be that Jesus chose this time, first, because he knew Peter: he knew the workings of his mind, thanks to the depth of relationship formed between them. Second, it appears that there was an element of divine timing about the whole thing. After all, Jesus points out that 'this was not revealed . . . by man, but by my Father in heaven'. Wouldn't it therefore be wise to take Jesus' lead here? Doesn't it make sense to allow the responsibility for convicting others of the ultimate truth to rest with God? Wouldn't life be so much easier if, instead of pointing out how far short of Jesus' standards people are falling as soon as we meet them, we got on with the business of offering a quality of companionship through which people are able to hear God's own conviction?

Problems and Solutions

I have a book full of questions we like to think non-Christians are just desperate to have answered: 'Why does God allow suffering?' 'Who invented God?' 'Do babies go to heaven?' Each question sits on top of a fresh page, with the following two sides being taken up with the 'answer'. I don't mind the fact that a book dealing with such questions has been written, but I feel a little unsure about these 'answers'. Yes, those questions do come up from time to time, but I've never been in a situation where a tasty, watertight answer to the 'why does God allow suffering' question has left someone on their knees saying the prayer. OK, so it might be a bit presumptuous, but things are different these days: truth just doesn't have the clout that it used to. As plenty of philosophers, sociologists and the like have pointed out, culture has undergone a massive shift from the hard and fast knowledge of absolute truth – where things were either right or wrong and that was that – to the shifting sands of relativism – where what's true for me may not be true for you. This shift has tripped up many an old-school evangelist, as a nice logical argument that *proves* the existence of Jesus no longer leads to the deal being done. 'Yup,' comes the reply, 'I can see that you believe in God, but I'm choosing to follow another path.' So, you see, we're desperately due an overhaul, our outlook on the world is long in need of a service. We cannot rely on arguments to win people over, and while this might seem like a shame (and it certainly means more work on our part) I'm struggling to see that type of approach modelled anywhere in Jesus' approach. To get back to the little book with

> neat answers to complex questions, I just
> wonder who it's written for: it certainly
> wouldn't cut much ice with the non-
> Christians I know. Perhaps it's just there to
> comfort those of us in the church who feel
> the need for a script to follow. And who can
> blame them?

BEING CONFORMED TO JESUS' IMAGE

When it comes to evangelism and forming
relationships with people who don't know Jesus,
we have often gone in hard and fast. Daze them
with a few jabs that reveal the truth about their
sin, get them on the ropes with the news of their
immediate need for work on their behaviour, and
then knock them out with a right hook that
leaves them in no doubt as to the amount of work
they have to put in before they look anything
like a Christian. While this approach certainly
grabs the attention, I wonder whether it fits in
with Jesus' approach. We have already seen that
he was just as concerned that people knew about
his companionship as that they knew about their
own sin. Also, it appears that the moment of
conviction – that revelation where it all finally

makes sense and we acknowledge Jesus for who he is – does not only ever need to be found at the start of a relationship with our heavenly Father. With Peter it took a while. If we're honest, I wonder whether things might look a little different if we adopted a similar approach in the church.

But despite the truth of all the above, we cannot ignore the fact that Jesus was concerned that the people around him did get to work on their lifestyles. With Jesus, there was the continual paradox that all were accepted as friends, but that his standards were continually encouraging people to reach higher. Perhaps this concept is not too alien to us; after all, the church has long been at home with pointing out faults and outlining the standards expected in new recruits. Sex, drugs, tithing, swearing – these are four of the most typical topics that may get addressed when nurturing a new Christian in the church. Getting to grips with these is, for many of us, a sure sign that a person is becoming more like Jesus.

Yet even the briefest of glimpses at the Gospels leaves us with plenty of questions about which issues were the ones that seemed to bother

Jesus. It's true, he was concerned that people's behaviour changed, yet we read that the areas to which he paid particular attention were those like the disciples' status-seeking, pride, bickering and anger. Take a look at Matthew 18:

At that time the disciples came to Jesus and asked, 'Who is the greatest in the kingdom of heaven?'

He called a little child and had him stand among them. And he said: 'I tell you the truth, unless you change and become like little children, you will never enter the kingdom of heaven. Therefore, whoever humbles himself like this child is the greatest in the kingdom of heaven.

'And whoever welcomes a little child like this in my name welcomes me. But if anyone causes one of these little ones who believe in me to sin, it would be better for him to have a large millstone hung around his neck and to be drowned in the depths of the sea.

'Woe to the world because of the things that cause people to sin! Such things must come, but woe to the man through whom they come! If your hand or your foot causes you to sin, cut it off and throw it away. It is better for you to enter life maimed or

> crippled than to have two hands or two feet
> and be thrown into eternal fire. And if your
> eye causes you to sin, gouge it out and
> throw it away. It is better for you to enter
> life with one eye than to have two eyes and
> be thrown into the fire of hell.
>
> Matthew 18:1–9

Jesus' choice of illustration was – we can assume – not chosen for the cute factor. Instead, by selecting a child as the winner of the 'Who is the Greatest?' competition, he manages to completely take the wind out of their sails. While this example remains one of the few where Jesus was harsh in his tone with the disciples, it comes after their relationship is well established, founded on trust and respect. The disciples knew that they belonged to Jesus and that he belonged to them. Funnily enough, that sort of security does wonders for a person's listening skills.

While we favour putting sexual sins in the spotlight, the four accounts of Jesus' life depict a man who spent more time talking about issues other than sexual immorality. For that you need to turn to the story of the woman at the well, where Jesus' prophetic insight acts as a stunning conversation opener. At other times Jesus seems far more concerned about money, power and ambition, as is clear from the story of him washing his disciples' feet during one of his last nights on earth:

> When he had finished washing their feet, he put on his clothes and returned to his place. 'Do you understand what I have done for you?' he asked them. 'You call me "Teacher" and "Lord", and rightly so, for that is what I am. Now that I, your Lord and Teacher, have washed your feet, you also should wash one another's feet. I have set you an example that you should do as I have done for you. I tell you the truth, no servant is greater than his master, nor is a messenger greater than the one who sent him. Now that you know these things, you will be blessed if you do them.'
>
> John 13:12–17

Here, late in the day, Jesus provides an image that will last for centuries: the Son of God taking on the role of a servant. This is no publicity stunt, no headline-grabber used merely for effect. By washing his disciples' feet Jesus was making a clear statement about the standards of behaviour he valued most: humility, self-sacrifice, generosity, anonymity.

Too often we can lead with a harsh message that alienates the listener. We get worried about standards of holiness and errors in behaviour long before we let people know that they really do have a place among us. We place on the agenda a series of tasks for people to compete before we allow them in, tasks which are often far wide of the mark set down by Jesus. For example, I can remember agonising for weeks about whether an open youth club my church was running – one that aimed to work alongside non-churched young people – should allow those that came along to smoke. Now, unhealthy as smoking may be, it would seem to be relatively far down on God's list of things for us to sort out. At the very least we can say that it would have been a little bit of a shame had we refused admittance to a relationship with Jesus on the grounds that an individual wanted to have a quiet cigarette while the relationship was being formed.

JESUS' CO-WORKERS

But none of this would be complete were it not for Jesus' knack of getting his disciples on board by having them work alongside himself. The Gospels indicate a clear pattern: Jesus performed the miracles while they watched, they then prayed for people while he watched, they went off and prayed for some more people and reported back to him afterwards, and finally they simply got on with it. Jesus was able to equip the team to be his co-workers by giving them jobs to do, by trusting them to make mistakes.

We should never underestimate the power that comes alongside a sense of purpose. Whether it's long-term unemployment or a crippling sense of unease at social gatherings, the effects of feeling as though we have nothing to contribute are easily noticeable. Which is why an old church that I used to belong to was really into jobs. There were hundreds of them to be done within the life of the church, from setting out chairs to running the tuck shop, from setting up the PA to collecting people who couldn't make their own way to the meetings. The plan was for everyone who wanted to be part of things to be able to see that they made a difference to the life of the church, that their contribution mattered. Sometimes it all got a bit much as people took on too many things, but at other times it was abundantly clear that by offering people the chance to become co-workers with us, the side-effects were potentially profound.

There was, for example, a team responsible for sorting out the décor at the church meetings. These creative types could do things with muslin that you'd never have thought possible, so we were a little surprised when they suggested that two particular young lads join their team. The two in question were rough, tough and most definitely not in touch with their feminine side. Draping muslin delicately over archways and doing wonders with soft lighting were not the first talents that sprang to mind when you met them. Not only were they decidedly un-décor-type people, they weren't Christians either. But they loved it. Week in and week out they'd scurry round the hall during the preparation time for each meeting, getting excited about their new-found love for artistic expression. And they did well, too, earning all the encouragement and praise that they received. But of all the good things about their involvement, the best was this: they started going along to the décor team prayer meetings, where they began to understand the connection between prayer, God and reality. And eventually they both became Christians.

For too long we as the church have worked to the agenda that people need to sort out their behaviour first, before they join the church – dealing with all those nasty, whiffy things like sex and drugs. Once they're all cleaned up they can get to grips with the task of learning to believe in God, and only when that has been achieved do we let them know that they belong. This clearly isn't working, as a glance at the church attendance figures or a look at the Jesus model will confirm. Instead, it occurs that the way Jesus related to people turned our agenda on its head. Instead of our rigid formula designed to get people as far down the path as possible before declaring them members, Jesus' way offered the chance to belong first, followed by the urge to believe. It was only then that the issue of behaviour was tackled.

This idea of turning our conventions on their head applies equally well to the way we disciple people. So far we've tended to lean on discipleship as a reward for good behaviour, setting a few minimum entry requirements before we open the doors. How about getting back to treating people as disciples even before they're signed up?

The interesting thing as you read the Gospels is that it's not always clear in what order Jesus' friends and disciples are working through the phases. These phases become less of a rigid programme and more of a continuum, one on which people are free to move about at various points. So while it might appear that Peter is still getting to grips with issues of whether he has been convicted of Jesus' true identity, he is settling down nicely into his role as co-worker with Christ.

Oh dear.

Why oh dear? Because this makes it hard for us. How can we be sure that things are running well, how can we be sure that the church is giving off the right message to all and sundry? If we allow any old bod to get up and take on positions of responsibility, what does it say about the importance of developing a mature relationship with Jesus?

Of course, such arguments are ridiculous; who are we to assume that we are the very pinnacle of spiritual perfection? Who are we to get in the way of God and set ourselves as the standard to be reached? Who are we to say that our ways are best? Yes, there are standards and there are challenges laid down by Jesus that go to the very core of our sinful nature, but we do others an injustice and the church some serious harm if we sign up to the deluded belief that telling people about Jesus is like selling membership to an exclusive club. All are included, all are invited. We are not bouncers. We are the servants.

A WORD ABOUT CHANGE

The story of the rich young ruler is probably one of the closest recorded encounters to our traditional view of an evangelistic encounter.

A certain ruler asked him, 'Good teacher, what must I do to inherit eternal life?'

'Why do you call me good?' Jesus answered. 'No-one is good – except God alone. You know the commandments: "Do not commit adultery, do not murder, do not steal, do not give false testimony, honour your father and mother." '

'All these I have kept since I was a boy,' he said.

When Jesus heard this, he said to him,

'You still lack one thing. Sell everything you have and give to the poor, and you will have treasure in heaven. Then come, follow me.'

When he heard this, he became very sad, because he was a man of great wealth. Jesus looked at him and said, 'How hard it is for the rich to enter the kingdom of God! Indeed, it is easier for a camel to go through the eye of a needle than for a rich man to enter the kingdom of God.'

Those who heard this asked, 'Who then can be saved?'

Jesus replied, 'What is impossible with men is possible with God.'

Peter said to him, 'We have left all we had to follow you!'

'I tell you the truth,' Jesus said to them, 'no-one who has left home or wife or brothers or parents or children for the sake of the kingdom of God will fail to receive many times as much in this age and, in the age to come, eternal life.'

Luke 18:18–30

I remember getting beaten up by these verses on a regular basis. For years I understood them to mean that unless I could give up everything – and that meant *everything* – then I was nothing more than a shallow, gold-digging Christian who had no right to call himself a friend of Jesus. And I suppose there is some truth in that interpretation, but we in the developed world focus on the economic aspect of the passage because we are rich. One day I heard an alternative take on it: that what Jesus offers the rich young ruler is the most amazing gift ever – friendship with him. 'Come and follow me,' he says, just as he did to Peter and Andrew, Philip and all the others. Jesus offers him relationship, the chance to get close, to learn, work and spend time with him. Jesus offers himself, but that was not what the man was looking for. He wasn't in the market for a genuine relationship with Jesus; he wanted a set of rules to live by, a system to guarantee eternal life, a magic formula that would leave the rest of his life intact. Unfortunately that's precisely what Jesus doesn't offer.

We find the idea of change difficult, especially when it involves the hard graft of working on attitudes, ambitions and other hidden recesses of our hearts. Of course, direct friendship with Jesus and the chance to be a part of his revolution was worth all the money in the world, but not to that young man. The price was too high.

Looking at Matthew 10 we can see how Jesus offered a unique insight into his theory of evangelism. We join the story as Jesus prepares to send out his disciples on an extended evangelistic mission. They will be gone some time, and the pep-talk condenses perfectly Jesus' philosophy of evangelism. He passes on his authority to perform supernatural signs and wonders just as they had seen him demonstrate, saying, 'freely you have received, freely give'. Later in the Bible John picks up on this idea, writing:

That which was from the beginning, which we have heard, which we have seen with our eyes, which we have looked at and our hands have touched – this we proclaim concerning the Word of life. The life appeared; we have seen it and testify to it, and we proclaim to you the eternal life, which was with the Father and has appeared to us. We proclaim to you what we have seen and heard, so that you also may have fellowship with us. And our fellowship is with the Father and with his Son, Jesus Christ.

1 John 1:1–3

This idea of only doing what we have seen Jesus do is a radical refocusing of our current concept of evangelism. Too often we try to redefine it, adding in bits from our own agenda. We chuck on all that stuff about sorting out behaviour and so on, about getting people spruced up and tidy before we allow them to join us, but are we sure that this method is one that we have seen modelled in the gospel?

Having hinted at this, Jesus gets down to basics:

These twelve Jesus sent out with the following instructions: 'Do not go among the Gentiles or enter any town of the Samaritans. Go rather to the lost sheep of Israel. As you go, preach this message: "The kingdom of heaven is near." Heal the sick, raise the dead, cleanse those who have leprosy, drive out demons. Freely you have received, freely give. Do not take along any gold or silver or copper in your belts; take no bag for the journey, or extra tunic, or sandals or a staff; for the worker is worth his keep.

'Whatever town or village you enter, search for some worthy person there and stay at his house until you leave. As you

> enter the home, give it your greeting. If the home is deserving, let your peace rest on it; if it is not, let your peace return to you. If anyone will not welcome you or listen to your words, shake the dust off your feet when you leave that home or town.
>
> Matthew 10:5–14

By telling the disciples to go without any economic back-up (no cash, no bedding and so on) Jesus is forcing them into an awkward position. They are soon to find themselves radically committed to their heavenly Father; if he fails to show they will end up at best embarrassed and at worst quite possibly dead. We too need to be prepared to step out of our comfort zones, to be prepared to take the gospel not just to our cosy friends, who we know accept and love us. Remember that moment when Jesus pushed Peter for an answer as to his own true identity? Well, what if the moment hadn't been right? What if the penny hadn't dropped or Peter had happened to be a little on the timid side that day? What if he had been feeling morose and sorry for himself? It could all have gone so wrong; but in modelling dependence on God, Jesus showed us that awkwardness does not mean that a situation is wrong.

But not only are they bound to end up dependent on God for their security: they will find themselves dependent on relationships that they form along the way. On arrival in the town the search would be on for the 'worthy person' with whom they would stay. And how was the Holy Spirit going to point that particular person out? Simple; it would be the person who talked to them. All it took was for someone to like the disciple in question, someone to offer a little hospitality and open up their home. And then what? 'Stay at this house until you leave,' says Jesus. Remind you of anything? Friendship, pure and simple.

But what are we to make of that line about how the disciples were to 'shake the dust' from their feet should they not get the right reception? Shaking the dust was a symbolic act that the Pharisees were fond of, and it declared a whole family unclean. To me it indicates that this whole deal of evangelism isn't just some wishy-washy affair. It is not inconsequential and it does matter. If someone chooses to reject the message of Christ then there are eventual consequences to their actions. Jesus' philosophy of evangelism revolved around relationships. The plan was this: go out and form relationships. Assume that they are going to work, but if they don't, if they reject both you and Jesus, then move on.

There are absolutes. There is a right and a wrong. There are decisions to be made, with consequences that follow. After all, that is why Jesus bothered to encourage us to form relationships in the first place. Following the Jesus model involves turning our preconceived ideas of structure and membership on their head. It also involves an awful lot more work. But the results . . . well, we'll come on to those next.

Case Study

I don't want to come over all cynical through this book, and I have to admit that I've done my own fair share of hardcore evangelism. For a period of time I was totally into the idea of hitting the streets with nothing but my Bible and a complete lack of care for how I may have appeared to others. As far as I was concerned I was on a mission from God and nothing could stop me. So, along with a few friends, I spent time going from door to door, talking to people about God. I'd go around tables in pubs to talk about the gospel, stand up in crowded tube trains and deliver a thirty-second message about the truth of Jesus' life and death. It was all good stuff done with good intentions, but it's only looking back on it now that I can begin to unravel the experiences. They were odd times, and they would always start with a warm-up, a pep-talk about how God was with us and no earthly power could stop the flow of the good news. During the activities themselves there was always a bit of a blank on the emotional scale, but I can clearly remember the sense of power and energy that flowed through once we had finished. We felt almost invincible, which was nice.

The only experience I can liken it to is telesales. I had a job one summer selling the usual (advertising) and the feelings were similar: nerves at the start which were turned into confidence during the pre-session pep-talk, taking on the world over the phone, bursting with self-belief, and walking home at the end of the day feeling like the world's greatest (or worst) salesman.

But I never knew anyone join the church. I never knew anyone become a disciple. Oh, there was one. I met him in a park and we chatted. I told him my story and he said the prayer. I gave him a Bible and he came along to a meeting. I never saw him again after that. Perhaps I even set him back rather than helped him move forward on his spiritual journey.

2

Words, Works and Wonders

Therefore I glory in Christ Jesus in my service to God. I will not venture to speak of anything except what Christ has accomplished through me in leading the Gentiles to obey God by what I have said and done – by the power of signs and miracles, through the power of the Spirit. So from Jerusalem all the way round to Illyricum, I have fully proclaimed the gospel of Christ. It has always been my ambition to preach the gospel where Christ was not known, so that I

> would not be building on someone else's
> foundation. Rather, as it is written: 'Those
> who were not told about him will see, and
> those who have not heard will understand.'
> This is why I have often been hindered from
> coming to you.
>
> Romans 15:17–22

The passage above finds Paul chewing the fat with a few evangelism anoraks keen to find out some of his top tips. According to this reply, Paul's goal of quality evangelism has been fully achieved and has been executed through the words he has spoken, the deeds he has done and the power of the Holy Spirit at work. If you happen to be a fan of the King James version of the Bible, you'll see that the translation lists as the three prongs of Paul's evangelistic strategy 'words . . . works . . . and wonders'. And as Paul seemed to do OK for himself, I wonder whether we too might be able to pick up a few tips from his particular model.

For too long we in the church have grasped the wrong end of this particular strategic stick. We have considered words, works and wonders as elements to be kept separate from each other.

And this is quite handy, as it has allowed us to develop a taste for a particular style without feeling guilty at our lack of adventure. So we have the option of putting all our interests in the art of delivering a good gospel message, or we search long and hard for the perfect tract, one that will have people falling to their knees at the quickest of readings. Or we might opt for the works side of things, where we take on the role of un-qualified and unpaid social workers. No other form of communication about Jesus is permitted than works of compassion, which can get a little tricky once people start to ask questions about why we behave in a certain way. Or we can choose to be real 'signs and wonders' merchants, believing in the power of the Holy Spirit above all others to change lives. Here we might take on the role of entertainer, believing that people need nothing more than to see something truly 'WOW' in order to secure their belief. But you know what? Separating them out like that doesn't do anyone any favours, least of all the very people we're trying to reach. Yet if we can hold them together, if we can discover the knack of being able to hold the three seemingly opposing styles in harmony, much as Paul did, then the results could be truly spectacular.

WORDS

I once had a job as a barman in a cocktail bar close to London's business centre. It was close to St Paul's, and at the time I was pleased enough that I'd managed to find work in so trendy a place – one with a neon sign and everything. Being full of my usual spiritual zeal and earnestness I'd made a number of pledges to God before starting my first shift. On leaving that evening, I was forced back to the boardroom of my mind to renegotiate some of my earlier promises. After just a few hours I was convinced that there was no possible chance of me being able to successfully tell the people who worked there about my faith. And as for substituting gospel tracts for those napkins on which the drinks were placed – well, that would clearly have not only got me fired but publicly lynched too. You see, the people I was now working with were serious non-Christians. And they were very good at it.

After a few weeks of working there I was travelling home on the train one night feeling guilty about my poor performance, especially as the old desire to actually do something positive among my colleagues had resurfaced. I felt God tell me simply to tell the truth, which was an odd thing as I wouldn't have said that I'd exactly been lying while I'd been working there. But as I thought about it things became a little clearer. Being a city bar it was closed over the weekend, so there was an element of the de-brief about the first shift on Monday. There people would go through their weekends, picking out the juicy bits and discarding the moments of tedium. When it came to my turn I realised that I tended to big up the Saturday activities and play down those that occurred on a Sunday. I'd say things like 'Yeah, Sunday was great . . . really relaxing to be with the family . . .' Which was true. But not completely true. My weekend story should have included a closing line about how much I had (or hadn't) enjoyed church on Sunday night, but somehow my voice always seemed to trail off before I got to that point. Which was convenient.

So I decided to change my ways and, whenever they asked me questions, to tell the truth. This seemed to work just fine, as for a few days people seemed to have lost their desire to talk to me, but one afternoon their shyness vanished.

'Where have you been?' asked Sarah, one of the other bar staff.

I had been doing what I usually did, which was to go up to St Paul's Cathedral and have a quiet time in one of the side chapels. So I told her where I'd been.

'Oh it's lovely up there. Did you do the whole tourist thing and take a tour?'

'Um,' I said, 'not quite.' And I explained about my time spent praying and reading my Bible. She looked at me blankly and then asked me the last question I had expected. 'Why do you pray?'

I couldn't think of a single reason. Eventually I mumbled something about how I felt that it helped, how I thought it was a good thing for me to be doing. She was interested and asked me what I prayed. I told her how I covered things like asking God for guidance and forgiveness, about praying for family, friends and work colleagues.

'So do you pray for us, then?'

'Yeah.'

'What do you pray?'

Again I gave another spectacularly unimpressive answer, as insipid words like 'nice', 'happy' and 'good' dribbled out of my mouth. I felt like the world's worst evangelist and had a sudden, frighteningly clear mental image of Billy Graham playing football with my head. But at least Sarah seemed interested, and she kept on coming up to me throughout the rest of the afternoon and evening to ask me further 'what' and 'how' and 'why' questions about my not-so-secret religious side.

She'd told others, too, and they quickly took an interest in things, which I thought was just a bit unfair; I was in this wretched deal with God whereby I had to answer if they asked. So I regularly volunteered to go down to the cellar to change the barrels just so that I could get some peace and quiet and pretend to be hiding my faith again.

Later, when the bar was packed, Sarah was carrying on her quick-fire questions about my faith as the song that had been playing came to an end. A sudden lull came over the bar just as she was halfway through her question:

'So David, are you one of those Christians that doesn't believe in sex?'

Everyone turned to look at me. I closed my eyes and wished for a miracle that would transport me far, far away.

* * *

When I had started the job hardly any of the staff had ever met a Christian. When I left I'd been able to talk to most of them and hand out a few Bibles. Why? Because our words matter, and when we commit to being real with people and telling the truth, God's kingdom comes a little nearer. Making that pact with God worked for me because I finally realised that talking about God to people who hardly knew him was not about slipping into a sales pitch, not about turning up the charm in an effort to schmooze someone into the kingdom. Instead, it was simply about being honest.

WORKS

Let's get this straight: by 'works' I don't mean 'effort'. We cannot sweat, squeeze or strain people into God's kingdom any more than we can argue them in. By 'works' I mean deeds of compassion, actions that speak louder than words, behaviour that takes its lead from Jesus' actions. Strangely, we have to be explicit about this, as the church in the West has struggled to get to grips with the idea that works of compassion are of themselves a decent evangelistic tool. We've come across all confused when others have suggested that to feed the hungry or clothe the poor is in itself an act that brings the kingdom of God closer to people. Sadly, unless the works have been accompanied by a 'let me tell you about Jesus' line, we've suspected that we've been wasting our time. But try telling that to Christians in certain developing countries and they'd look at you like you're deranged. For many who face poverty so frequently and in such severity, it is blindingly obvious that if the hungry are fed then God's good news is being preached. If people are home-less then the good news of Jesus surely is that they have somewhere to live.

In attempting to separate works from spread-ing the news of Jesus, we've got into evangelism that has little to do with people's personal needs, as well as meeting people's personal needs in a way that is wholly unrelated to evangelism. Both of these strike me as a shame, especially when I consider the kind of work that a friend of mine does with long-term unemployed people in a large city. This project has the highest success rate of any of its kind in the country, and has been patted on the back by the government and told that it is a model project. How? Because they

don't only offer job-related training, but by forming relationships they invest in every single
person who joins them so that their confidence
grows in every area of their lives. This means they
wind up talking to people about all manner of
issues, from debt to family, education to parent-
ing, and at every turn try to offer quality relationships that can make a difference. It's wonderful
to see Christians work together in this way, but
deep down perhaps we all know that there are
some who would question whether a project
as committed and generous as this really is
evangelistic. Why? Because there are no words
being used, no tracts being handed out at the
start of each course.

I once met some members of a university
Christian Union who had recently hit on
success with their annual mission. Like many
CUs, they felt that they wanted to do something
each year to reach out and spread the good news
among their fellow students. For years they had
hired in the big-name evangelist and the band,
handed out flyers in the daytime and held gigs
and debates in the evenings, and while things
had worked just fine, one year they decided
to ring the changes and opt for something

WORDS, WORKS AND WONDERS   71

completely different. So they chose a specific
developing country, found out about projects
within the country that were working with the
poorest people, and generally got themselves
well acquainted with the specific problems and
potential solutions for the people in need. Next
they produced a range of T-shirts, postcards and
so on and launched a university-wide campaign
to help raise both funds and awareness about
the plight of the people. The campaign ran for
a week and involved loads of people – only a
few of whom were Christians – and made a
huge impact on campus life. At the end of each
day all those involved would go back to the
bar and talk things over, plan for the next day
and generally unwind. By the end of the
week-long mission the CU saw more people
become Christians than through the previous
three missions combined. Why? Because the
Christians stopped being known as people who
talked and started to be known as people who
did.

[Now, this section on works has deliberately
been kept a little on the short side: not because it
all sounds like a bit too much hard graft, but due
to the simple fact that all my ideas got used up in

Upwardly Mobile, a book that deals with the theme in greater depth.]

Problems and Solutions

You see, sometimes this evangelism thing all feels too impersonal. It's as if we have to drop our personality – our likes, dislikes, opinions and character – and start to spout the party line. At times I've felt as if, midway through a quiet drink with a friend, I ought to have put down my pint, adopted a pleasant yet serious expression and 'got down to business' by explaining the real reason for my being there. And what if my real reason for being there was because I wanted to hang out with a friend? Not good enough: at times it feels like the real reason for socialising with non-Christians is so that they can become Christians. Well, I'm sorry, but that won't do. If all our friendships have a 'save by' date on them, if all our social gatherings need to taper expertly to a moment where we can dim the lights, turn down the music and whisper sweet spiritual nothings in our friend's ear, then count me out. Come to think of it, you could probably count out Jesus, Paul and the early church, too: for them, relationships were valid in themselves. They were neither conditional on progress nor fake about truth. Yes, Jesus told his disciples to shake the dust and all that, but that was more about relationships that had failed to take off than friends who were unwilling to listen. At the end of the day, there's got to be a way that I can show, tell and inspire people about the God I love without having to leave my personality at the door. Hasn't there?

WONDERS

As a product it's not hard to see some of the flaws present within Christianity. Why, by the process of a simple tweak here and a nip and tuck there, the whole thing could have so much more pzazz, be far easier to handle and feel so much more comfortable. If only we could make it so that regular Christian life was like the isolated pockets of fired-up frenzy we all love so much when it comes round to the annual Christian festival. There our doubts fly away, our spirits soar and our consciences wash a whiter shade of white. There's a miracle at the end of every meeting, a tale of victory being told at every queue and just enough heroes up on the platform to wow, sparkle and give us all something to aim for. Life at these times is easy, far easier than the harsh reality of home. There the miracles certainly are not waiting behind every closed door, and the supermarkets are most certainly not the venues for powerful moves of the Holy Spirit. We may have been used to seeing wonderful moves of God at the festival, but as soon as we're back home the idea of seeing God's power in action in any place other than the church can be frankly odd.

It's sad to admit it, but the whole area of wonders – works of the Holy Spirit – is yet another that we have pensioned off away from the subject of everyday evangelism. We might admit to it working for a few individuals up there on the platform, but when it comes to us, most often we find the prospect of praying for a miracle in the middle of the pub nothing short of embarrassing.

Once, when I was involved in a church working in one of the more deprived areas of London, there was a time when we'd get regular visits to our outreach evenings from a particularly rough group of lads. They'd been in and out of police custody, and most had spent time in young offenders' institutions. Naturally they scared the life out of me. One particular night they turned up and were being unusually aggressive. Being a generous and balanced leader, I decided to send someone else over to deal with them, and from my position cowering behind a bench I watched as two of the more petite women on the team went up to them. They talked, but I couldn't hear their precise words. As I watched I saw one of the women raise her hand, looking as if she was about to slap one of the lads. Visions of a horribly quick and one-sided fight flashed across my mind, and I decided that there was nothing for it but for me to step in and offer myself as a martyr. Thankfully my blood wasn't needed that day: by the time I had walked across, the woman had prayed for one of the biggest lads, who swooned a bit and then fell over. His friends looked on, not knowing whether to fight, laugh or run off.

'That was fantastic!' he said after a few seconds on the floor. 'What was it?'

'That,' said the woman, 'was God.'

All his friends made gentle 'oooooh' noises and looked back at their mate.

'Do it again,' came his reply.

Faced with the option of having him back up and pushing people about, getting the lad dosed up on the Holy Spirit for the night seemed like a very attractive option, even if it felt a little bit like a side-show attraction. After he'd been up and down a couple of times his mates wanted to have a go too, and by the time the hour was up they had all 'had a dose', as they put it.

And they came back. Week after week they turned up to the meetings, and we got to know them. Their stories were told and we began to understand a little of what they had been through. It might not have been the most comfortable of experiences at first, but it brought home the message to all of us in the church: that sometimes we simply have to get on with the business of trusting God and expect him to move in power. Simple.

Perhaps it is this type of risk, this danger of suffering extreme embarrassment, that prevents us from signing up fully to the workings of the Holy Spirit. After all, it could so easily have gone horribly wrong for my friend as she started to pray for the tough lad: nothing might have happened to him and the whole relationship would have taken a slide even further back down the hill. But isn't that the point? If we want to see God do amazing things, doesn't it make sense that we put ourselves in positions where we are fully dependent on him to work? Isn't it simply a matter of saying something like 'Can I pray for you?' They can only say 'no'. Whether it 'works' or not is up to God, and it's bound to get a few questions going.

Having spent a few weeks coming to our outreach evenings in a local pub, eventually the lads wanted to come along to our church services. Which was interesting. As soon as they saw the ministry going on at the end of the service they started to get excited.

'That bloke just punched that woman!' they'd shout from the back.

It took some explaining to make it clear that what was going on was not people hitting each other but God moving in much the same way as he had when the lads themselves had fallen over.

'So can we go and watch?'

The thought of seven colossal lads from Deptford crowding around someone receiving ministry somehow didn't quite seem to fit with the established protocol, but when I started to um and ah about their request they complained that it was obviously a fake. So they went up and watched. And they commented. Loudly.

'Go on, then,' they'd tell the person who was getting ready to do the praying, 'knock him out.' Then, turning to the person who had come up for ministry, they'd offer a comforting, 'Don't worry, it's only God.'

Even looking back to those days now, I'm tempted to think of the circumstances as odd: seven hard lads staring at people during ministry, challenging people to 'hit them with God' and generally experiencing the power of the Holy Spirit long before they knew anything about being a Christian. But why *should* it feel odd? Why should that be unusual? Surely it's a shame that we've removed wonders from our evangelism, reserving them as treats not to be opened until a contract has been signed. And isn't this the heart of the problem with our approach to evangelism: that we have managed to isolate, extract and sanitise the whole process. We've made it into a programme, we've written a script and we've developed a technique. Worst of all, we've moved the whole deal far, far away from the essential truth: that evangelism is about introducing people to a relationship with Jesus. Paul did that any way he could – through words, works and wonders – but for us some of these aspects have become strangers.

It wasn't only Paul who adopted a multi-faceted, relationship-oriented approach to spreading the gospel. It doesn't take that long spent flicking through the book of Acts to work out that the growth of the early church was based on a similar foundation:

> They devoted themselves to the apostles' teaching and to the fellowship, to the breaking of bread and to prayer. Everyone was filled with awe, and many wonders and miraculous signs were done by the apostles. All the believers were together and had everything in common. Selling their possessions and goods, they gave to anyone as he had need. Every day they continued to meet together in the temple courts. They broke bread in their homes and ate together with glad and sincere hearts, praising God and enjoying the favour of all the people. And the Lord added to their number daily those who were being saved.
>
> Acts 2:42–7

Discussion, sacrificial living and miracles: three core ingredients that fertilised the growth of the early church. Somehow they managed to combine the more formal platform-based evangelistic activities with their own personal responsibilities, and perhaps we too could do with learning how to do the same. It can be too easy for us to switch off and consider that evangelism is either something that other people – other more gifted public speakers – do for us or something that we do only when we have to, but such a methodology fits neither Jesus' model nor Paul's.

If we're going to be really honest with ourselves here we ought to admit that it is in this area of personal evangelism that we should be seeing the most growth. Sure, the big events and missions are still important and will bring fresh people into contact and relationship with Jesus, but the church's best chance of growth surely lies with us, the majority. Whether together or on our own, we have the potential for following Paul's lead and relying on all three aspects of evangelism. Instead of scheduling in monthly 'Let me tell you about why you're going to hell' type conversations with our acquaintances, we can start to live lives that get people asking questions. Being honest in our replies will add further layers to the relationship, and relying on God to deliver all that flash stuff – well, doesn't that relieve the pressure from us just a little?

And what are we evangelising for, anyway? Is it for a conversion? Are we in it for the head-count, to see how many contracts we can get signed in a certain period of time? Or are we following Jesus' model, are we aiming to produce disciples, people who have a deepening relationship with Jesus? Of course, if we're choosing to offer this second option it will take a whole lot more time and is best not taught from a textbook but shown by example. Deciding to commit to quality relationships with people reframes our whole outlook on evangelism: out goes the emphasis on quantity and in comes a new commitment to quality; we say goodbye to the quick fix and welcome the search for the truth; we put down our defences and we welcome people to get to know the real us.

Case Study

Caroline was one of those good Christians who grew up in a good Christian home, went to a good Christian church and lived an altogether good Christian life. She didn't drink, smoke, flirt outrageously or take her faith too lightly. She was a model member of the church youth group, one the leaders lost no sleep about. And then she left. No warning. No goodbyes. Just a disappearance. Of course, she was still around, bumping into people at school and at the shops on a Saturday afternoon, but as far as church was concerned – well, it was as if it had never happened. People from the group tried to get in touch. They wanted to find out what was wrong and whether they could do anything to help her through this crisis of faith, but she hung up their calls, binned their e-mails or stared blankly past their concerned frowns.

If they could have seen her diaries they would have given up the search for answers: within the pages was a stream of bitterness and frustration, the real story about a faith that had been based on nothing more than feelings. One day she had realised something profound: that the feelings were no longer there. So she did the only thing that made sense and cut God out of her life.

Years went by, and occasional conversations with ex-church members became less and less frequent. Strangely, she began to find herself thinking about going back. Was her faith based completely on feelings? Wasn't there the chance that just one small particle had been based on something true? Might part of it have been something other than an illusion?

While most of the people she bumped into from church still looked awkward, there were a couple of people who had stuck by her throughout her years away from church and God. These had been the only two who hadn't tried to persuade her to go back, the only ones who had allowed her to rant and rave about all the things she was struggling with. One summer they invited her on holiday with them: it was a church affair but if she went along she would be doing them a favour by helping out with some of the jobs they had to do there. She joined them and found herself surprised at how much fun she was having. She was amazed at how the new people she met were interested in her, about how they didn't judge or assume things about her. So she hung around the church meetings that were taking place on the camp, eyeing the proceedings up, wary of getting caught in the emotional whirl again. No one was fussed whether she went in or not, and neither of her friends questioned her about whether she was coming back to church. On the last day, quietly, without anyone knowing, she prayed again for the first time in years. She asked God for help. That night she went to sleep feeling, for the first time ever, like she was coming home.

3

The Early Church

Quality over quantity? Disciples over converts? All sounds a bit like hard work, doesn't it? And anyway, are we really so sure that it actually works? I mean, the examples of Jesus and Paul *are* from the church's infancy: surely we'd see a different story emerging over time?

It's true that things have changed, that the church's strategy for filling the pews has undergone some reasonably extensive surgery over the centuries. But it's the extent of that change that causes the surprise. Even the briefest of glimpses of the life of the early church has the potential to unsettle and confound. Their approach was about as different to ours today as is possible. And you know what? It worked.

We're talking about the growth of Christianity from the tail end of Paul's ministry up to the early stages of the fourth century. This period is the filling in a time-sandwich that shaped the church in some profound ways. At one end (in the middle of the AD 60s) was the wholesale persecution of the Christians by the Roman emperor Nero, while at the other (in AD 312) was the conversion of the Roman emperor Constantine. After that Christianity was the official religion of the Roman empire and things changed. In came Christendom and out went the underground movement; for some the faith became a tool for social advancement, while for those beforehand it had been a way of life.

But we're getting ahead of ourselves here. This period before the official recognition of Christianity is absolutely pivotal to the growth of the church. After the initial birth of the movement as described in the New Testament, its infancy was dangerous, uncertain and often at grave risk. But you know what? The church was an absolute winner. With its back to the wall it still managed to faithfully spread the message of the gospel throughout the Middle East and the Mediterranean, with as much as 10 per cent of the population of the Roman empire being converted within 300 years. That kind of growth is astounding, especially for us today, when we appear to be leaking members like we're going out of fashion.

So the logical next step is to ask some simple questions: why did the pre-Christendom church do so well? What did they have that we don't? Whatever it is, can we borrow a bit? So here we go:

WHY DID THE PRE-CHRISTENDOM CHURCH DO SO WELL?

Tip-top preaching on street corners . . . easily accessible services . . . an acceptance of all who wanted to join . . . the church bore none of those features which we assume are on the list marked 'Essentials' when it comes to church characteristics. In fact, thanks to the political heat that threatened to overwhelm those caught preaching the outlawed message, their approach was wholly different to ours. There was 'little, if any, direct preaching to the masses',[1] not much in the way of missions – and as for prayer for conversion, 'the Christians prayed for the prosperity of and peace of people, but scarcely for their conversion'.[2]

Perhaps even more shocking is the revelation that the steroid growth of the church wasn't even caused by people coming into contact with their radical worship sessions. The plain truth is that the pagans *weren't allowed* to join in with the Christians' worship services. And even more amazingly, they weren't allowed to join in the life-blood of the services (communion) until they had completed what amounted to a three-year induction programme. Until they had completed this extensive discipleship course they were only allowed to stay in church for the sermon, getting kicked out before the prayers, kiss of peace and communion.

Ah, you might say, but what about Paul: didn't he make some reference to tailoring the service so that when 'outsiders or unbelievers enter' they will 'not say you are out of your mind'? Yes, he did (in 1 Corinthians 14:23) but that was before the persecution of the Christians in the mid AD

60s. The simple truth is that the church was seen as a threat to those in power, and after Nero turned up the heat it was far too dangerous to allow just anybody into the services.

This leads us to an uncomfortable conclusion: that there was no link between worship and evangelism. Come to think of it, if you're judging it by our current models of preaching to strangers, getting them introduced to the Holy Spirit or making snappy gospel presentations, it's kind of questionable whether we would recognise any form of evangelism in their actions at all. So should we pack up right now? Is this our cue to bail out of the worship service, to cease putting any effort into communicating with God or sharing it with others? Of course not. But how, when on the surface they seemed to make it so difficult for people to become Christians, did the pre-Christendom church manage to build up so many of them?

The members of the early church didn't hide their worship because it was naff: they hid it because it was important. Like all true worship, theirs made a difference to their lives. It transformed them, brought them closer to God and to each other and underpinned their whole approach to being outwardly active. And while we might not recognise some of their less accessible approaches to non-believers, there are a number of historical sources from the time that point to the kind of lives people lived. A pagan guy named Caecilius reported that the Christians were the type who were 'silent in public, chattering in corners'.[3] Christians were subtle, dressing the same as everybody else, keeping a low profile and generally causing surprise when others found out about their faith. Remember, this was not to do with shame but with safety. And it obviously worked well for them.

They lived in a highly divisive society. The many structures and levels meant that there were plenty at the bottom of the pile who remained poor while the wealthy ones at the top increased the gap. But the Christians lived against this, with the rich members giving generously through the church's common fund to help the poorer members. It's like that old 'everything in common' idea we read about at the start of the book of Acts, and in terms of causing a stir there's nothing quite like putting your money where your mouth is. They gave money to strangers, cared for the graves of the dead and extended their generosity to those who knew nothing of what they believed.

The wonderful truth about this crucial phase in the church's growth is that, as Alan Kreider puts it,

> The Christians were aware that the life of their communities was remarkable; and they wanted to live in such a way that this was visible enough to draw people to faith and freedom in Christ. 'Beauty of life,' one of them contended, '. . . causes strangers to join the ranks . . . We do not talk about great things: we live them.'[4, 5]

The early church looked not for converts but for disciples. At the heart of its strategy for growth lay a system of discipleship that was even more rigorous than the education offered by universities today. Here's the deal: believers who had established contact with pagans and become friends, if they were convinced of their seriousness, would take them to one of the church's daily early morning meetings. There the pagans would be introduced to a *catechist* (a discipler or trainer), whose job was to interview both the believer who was sponsoring the pagan and the candidate themselves. The questions were rigorous, probing for reasons that might make them ripe for rejection. As the manual of the time (*Apostolic Tradition*) points out, their marital state, employment and attitudes were all taken into consideration during this weeding-out process. Even once they had got through, the commitment demanded of both the future Christian and the person who had introduced them to the faith in the first place was great: in some areas both would visit the church house every single day before work for an hour of study. There they would examine the Bible, listen to a talk given by the trainer, probably discuss it at length, pray, and receive a blessing before leaving. This would go on for three years, during which they were expected to live like Christians, feeding, sacrificing and living holy lives. It was only after all this that they could be considered for baptism, following which they would be allowed to join the church as a full member, sharing in communion, the peace and receiving the gifts of the Holy Spirit.

Problems and Solutions

Let's talk about passion. You know what it's like when something marvellous has happened in your life, how hard it can be to keep it a complete secret? Well, that's how it ought to be with Jesus and us, right?

Well, I'm not so sure. Of course, in one way the answer is a complete '*Yes!*' – I mean, of course having a relationship with Jesus is something worth chatting about. But this idea of bubbling over with excitement, of being so spine-tinglingly-thrilled-about-all-things-to-do-with-our-faith-that-we-just-have-to-shout-about-it – is that really what it's like for us? I'll let you in on a secret here: not every day in my life is a laughter-filled stroll through corn-kissed meadows, hand in hand with Jesus. Sometimes I feel so far away from him, so very much surrounded by ME, that I worry that if I opened my mouth and told people what I thought about things they'd probably shrivel away in horror. And this is my problem: I feel as if I've got to shoe-horn myself into a mode of evangelism that blatantly doesn't fit. After all, Christianity's main aim is not that our lives become free of all traces of pain, frustration and suffering, so what good is it to pretend otherwise?

And what of the solution? Well, I wonder whether it's as simple as this: we need to be real with people, and that means sharing something of the struggles as well as the excitements. Of course, this doesn't mean that we should start accosting strangers in the supermarket with tales of woe and despair; but those that we're closest to, the ones who share their passions and pains with us – perhaps we can treat them with integrity, authenticity and respect.

WHAT DID THEY HAVE THAT WE DON'T?

In a way we've answered this already, but the differences between our way of church and that which existed almost two thousand years ago are worth drawing out. The early crew were radically committed to expanding and growing their movement, but their methods seem almost alien to our own. Where we have a sweet tooth for the quick sell, they went for the long-term nurture. While we like to win people over with slick presentations that force them to consider

Christianity as relevant and cool, our ancestors held back on the entertainment. We like to shy away from making judgements about a person's lifestyle before they join us; they put up barriers to people joining.

Here's another thing they had: persecution. While not every Christian lived in fear of imminent death, the sacrifice of the martyrs had a secure place in the back of most Christians' minds. They did live under a threat of danger. Perhaps for us in the West it's impossible to comprehend what that might feel like, but this doesn't mean that their experiences lose any of their relevance to our own situation. Existing in an environment where faith brought with it certain consequences, perhaps many of them took things a little more seriously than we do. Too often we sell people Christianity as if it were a cosy country club, a health spa with fringe benefits. Ever since Constantine got converted and Christianity became a decent enough badge to wear, a sign of respectability, the church has been used by some as a hobby – something *nice*, not too challenging yet pleasant enough for an hour on a Sunday. Life or death decisions? No chance.

This is not my way of suggesting that we all ought to employ hit-men to pepper our services with random knee-cappings and free-form terror. But perhaps we do need to recognise the fact that Christianity is seen by the majority of non-Christians as irrelevant and lacking in purpose. The solution? How about taking a tip from the early bods and signing up for a bit of that eye-catching lifestyle? *Apostolic Tradition* suggested that, before baptism, the (not so) new recruits should: 'Let their life be examined. Have they lived good lives when they were catechumens [trainees]? Have they honoured the widows? Have they visited the sick? Have they done every kind of good work?'[6]

After all, if it was an entry requirement back in those days, shouldn't those of us who are already in the church right now be reaching the same standards?

WHATEVER IT IS, CAN WE BORROW A BIT?

The early church is more than just a great story: it's inspirational and holds the key to our future success as a church in the West. Yes, there are cultural differences that probably don't translate that well, but the positive lessons far outweigh the oddities.

Theirs was not a strategy for church growth that was driven by numbers. Where we act as double-glazing salespeople – making a contact and then bringing them along to church where the real professionals can get to work on signing them up quickly – our brothers and sisters from way back took on the role of parents. Conversion was not a five-minute affair that followed a decent talk. It was a massive commitment on the part of the church, the new believer and the Christian who had brought them along in the first place. After all, just how many early-morning training sessions could you attend before work? No, the simple fact is that they looked for disciples, not converts, they invested in people, not marketing campaigns, and they were in it for the long haul, not just the snap decision. Could we do with borrowing some of that?

And what about the church itself? It seems to me that you can't read about the life of the early church without coming across the word 'community'. It's simply impossible to separate the action of the Sunday meetings from the lifestyles of the members. Church really was about being outwardly active, about nurturing a lifestyle that did good, that spread the gospel, extended the kingdom and caused people to ask questions. Might that go down well with the people around us?

But isn't this anti-worship? Aren't we running the risk of saying that worship is unimportant? Of course not, and the fact that the early Christians guarded it so carefully underlines the fact that they valued it so very highly. Still, it strikes me that we've fallen into an unfortunate trap of late. By placing (nearly) all our evangelistic eggs in the basket of experience – by getting people along to the church service and encouraging them to experience God for real as we pray for their conversion – we have begun to lose faith in the power of other ways in which people can be impacted by God. You see, our lifestyles *can* make a difference. We *can* cause people to ask, to ponder and to investigate. Christianity is not dependent on people getting the right feelings before they notice a difference about us. And what's more, our worship *is* important: it can change lives. Perhaps we ought to be giving a little more space to exploring how our faith affects the 24/7 and not just the Sunday service.

So where do we go from here? Back to bed feeling guilty? Out to the fancy-dress shop to secure a decent toga for our next encounter with non-believers? Here's how Alan Kreider ended his examination of the pre-Christendom church: 'I believe that worship can nurture people today, as it nurtured the pre-Christendom Christians, to be missionaries in our culture.'[7]

Could we do with getting hold of a bit of that? Believe it. Dream it. Live it.

Top Tips for the Outwardly Active
Pray for your friends every day

Notes

1 Arthur Darby Nock, *Conversion* (Clarendon Press, Oxford, 1933)
2 Y. Congar, *Kyriakon: Festschrift Johannes Quasten* (Aschendorff, Munster, 1970)
3 Minucius Felix, *Octavius* 8.4
4 Minucius Felix, *Octavius* 31.7, 38.5
5 Alan Kreider, *Worship and Evangelism in Pre-Christendom* (Grove Booklets, 1995)
6 *Apostolic Tradition*, 21
7 Alan Kreider, *Worship and Evangelism in Pre-Christendom* (Grove Booklets, 1995)